ORCA
FOOTPRINTS

Rush Hour

NAVIGATING OUR GLOBAL TRAFFIC JAM

ERIN SILVER

ORCA BOOK PUBLISHERS

Library and Archives Canada Cataloguing in Publication
Title: Rush hour : navigating our global traffic jam / Erin Silver.
Names: Silver, Erin, 1980- author.
Series: Orca footprints.
Description: Series statement: Orca footprints | Includes
bibliographical references and index.
Identifiers: Canadiana (print) 20210247703 |
Canadiana (ebook) 20210247800 | ISBN 9781459827752 (hardcover) |
ISBN 9781459827769 (PDF) | ISBN 9781459827776 (EPUB)
Subjects: LCSH: Traffic flow—Juvenile literature. | LCSH: Traffic congestion—
Juvenile literature. | LCSH: Traffic density—Juvenile literature. |
LCSH: Traffic flow—Environmental aspects—Juvenile literature. |
LCSH:Traffic congestion—Environmental aspects—Juvenile literature. |
LCSH: Traffic density—Environmental aspects—Juvenile literature.|
LCSH: Traffic congestion—Prevention—Juvenile literature.
Classification: LCC HE336.T7 S55 2022 | DDC j388.3/1—dc23

Library of Congress Control Number: 2021941349

Summary: This nonfiction book for middle-grade readers looks at the
evolution of traffic, how it's affecting the environment, and practical
things young people can do to help. Illustrated with photographs.

Orca Book Publishers is committed to reducing the consumption of
nonrenewable resources in the production of our books. We make
every effort to use materials that support a sustainable future.

Orca Book Publishers gratefully acknowledges the support
for its publishing programs provided by the following
agencies: the Government of Canada, the Canada Council
for the Arts and the Province of British Columbia through
the BC Arts Council and the Book Publishing Tax Credit.

Front cover images by DuKai photographer/Getty Images
and DANNY HU/Getty Images
Back cover images by Hung_Chung_Chih/Getty Images,
Jose A. Bernat Bacete/Getty Images, andrey_l/Shutterstock.com
Design by Teresa Bubela
Layout by Dahlia Yuen
Edited by Kirstie Hudson

Printed and bound in Canada.

25 24 23 22 • 1 2 3 4

*Traffic is a major problem in cities around the
world. Shanghai (pictured here) is no exception.*
ASIA-PACIFIC IMAGES STUDIO/GETTY IMAGES

To Scott, my GPS. Thanks for taking this ride with me.

Contents

CHAPTER ONE:
COLLISION COURSE

CHAPTER TWO:
GO WITH THE FLOW

CHAPTER THREE:
DRIVING INTO THE FUTURE

CHAPTER FOUR:
HOW KIDS CAN HELP DRIVE CHANGE

Introduction

As the sun sets in Toronto, traffic fills the major highways.
BRADY BAKER/GETTY IMAGES

Red taillights as far as I could see. All the way up the highway, they blinked and flashed as drivers hit their brakes. Stop. Creep forward. Stop. Creep forward again. My son squirmed in the back seat.

"Mom, I'm gonna be late. Can't you go any faster?"

I glanced at my GPS. At this rate there was no way he'd be on time for baseball practice, and there was nothing I could do. I was stuck in **rush hour** on Canada's widest and busiest highway. "We'll never make it on time," I muttered.

Everywhere I looked—as far as I could see—there were cars, sport utility vehicles (SUVs), trucks and buses. I was stuck behind a long orange school bus that belched a big black cloud of exhaust right onto my windshield. "That bus is disgusting," said my son as the dark haze engulfed our car.

If I could see the smog from a bus and a nearby truck and an old sputtering car just up ahead, imagine all the **pollution** I couldn't see. Rush hour was bad for baseball, but how were all these **idling** cars affecting our health?

We made it to baseball practice. We were late, but at least my son got some time at bat. All that *traffic* congestion made me think. There are a billion cars driving on roads all over the world. In some countries, pollution from cars, trucks and school buses makes the air so unbreathable that kids can't play outdoors. The chemicals released from our vehicles also hurt our planet. Transportation, especially personal vehicles, is now the leading cause of **greenhouse gas emissions** in many cities all over the world.

And we're all contributing to the problem.

You can't drive a car. You don't decide what car your family buys. You can't make sure that school buses aren't clouding the air with soot. But kids are facing an environmental crisis unlike anything we've seen before. This is the time to start thinking about changing our habits and making healthier decisions. One day *Rush Hour* readers will be able to drive, but I hope that by then maybe you won't want or need to drive as often. Maybe you will have found a better way.

Pollution from tailpipes is bad for people and the planet.
JOSE A. BERNAT BACETE/GETTY IMAGES

Kids can't drive, but they can help steer change in the right direction.
INK DROP/SHUTTERSTOCK.COM

CHAPTER ONE

Collision Course

It's fun to think about what traffic might look like in the future. There could be flying cars and traffic lights in the sky. Maybe there will be traffic jams in the air. Police drones might give out speeding tickets. But before we get too far ahead of ourselves, let's take a closer look at how transportation evolved.

BEFORE THERE WERE CARS, THERE WERE CANOES

Believe it or not, people didn't always get around in cars. For thousands of years Indigenous Peoples in North America have traveled on rivers and lakes by canoe in summer. In winter they follow frozen waterways. When the British and French settlers and soldiers arrived in North America in the 16th and 17th centuries, they used the same routes. This was how food, fur, spices, metal and wood made their way across the continent. These methods of transporting goods helped the economy grow.

Today we canoe for recreation, but it wasn't too long ago that boats like this were a main form of transportation.
WASIM ISLAM

Hold on to your horses. Before cars, people used horses and wagons to get around.

GIDDYUP! GETTING AROUND WITH HORSES AND BUGGIES

Imagine riding a bicycle along bumpy, unpaved roads. You'd probably toss your cookies! That's what it was like in many places around the world in the 1700s and 1800s. Roads were so bad that people preferred to travel on horseback or by foot rather than in a wagon. Wagons were usually homemade, the wheels made from oak-tree trunks, and were pulled by horses or oxen. It wasn't a comfortable or safe ride. And it probably smelled bad too!

Good roads were needed to move soldiers to fight military battles and to expand trade routes, so the government paid professionals to build better roads. These routes spread farther and farther, connecting cities and, eventually, whole continents. The timing was perfect—soon "horseless buggies" would be invented.

PIT STOP

Have you ever heard the term *horsepower*? It was invented to compare the power of steam engines with the power of workhorses. Now it's used to talk about engines. The higher the horsepower, the faster a car can accelerate. Early cars, like the 1920 Ford Model T roadster with a turtle deck, had about 22.5 horsepower. Compare that to the car with the most horsepower today, the Bugatti Chiron Super Sport 300+. It has 1,600 horsepower.

This is my son's favorite car. Don't blink or you might miss it driving by!

ROAD TRIP

Even though the assembly line revolutionized the auto industry by increasing the number of cars that could be produced, workers hated it. They had to stand there doing the same repetitive job over and over again for nine hours a day, without proper breaks. People quit so often that in 1914 Henry Ford made an announcement at his plant. Instead of paying workers $2.34 for a nine-hour day, he would now pay $5 for an eight-hour day. Even though the job didn't improve, the extra pay kept workers on the job.

People worked hard on Ford assembly lines to produce cars for a growing number of drivers.

FROM THE COLLECTIONS OF THE HENRY FORD

VROOM-VROOM! THE INVENTION OF THE CAR

When Karl Benz designed an engine powerful enough to move people, the future of transportation changed forever. In 1886 Benz sold 25 Patent-Motorwagen cars to customers. At first only a few wealthy people had them. These cars were used just like go-karts—for fun. Cars were expensive, unreliable and even dangerous. There also weren't proper rules or safety regulations.

But as people found less expensive ways to make cars in the early 1900s, the auto industry took off. The first *assembly line* started moving at the Ford plant near Detroit in 1913. It wasn't long before motorized vehicles were zipping along roads. Soon the horse and buggy were replaced by cars. Sales in Canada grew by almost 800 times in just over 20 years.

This chart shows how quickly cars became the main form of transportation.

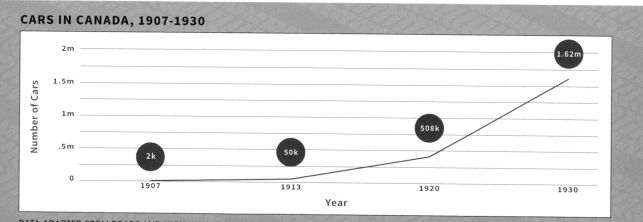

CARS IN CANADA, 1907-1930

Number of Cars (vertical axis): 0, .5m, 1m, 1.5m, 2m

- 1907: 2k
- 1913: 50k
- 1920: 508k
- 1930: 1.62m

Year (horizontal axis)

DATA ADAPTED FROM ROADS AND HIGHWAYS, THE CANADIAN ENCYCLOPEDIA, C.W. GILCHRIST, FEB 7 2006

CHAOS IN THE STREETS

Picture this: you're in the gym with the entire school, and everyone decides to play a different game at once. Little kids are hula-hooping next to big kids shooting hoops. Some are playing floor hockey, and others are playing dodgeball. There are no teachers or referees to make sure everyone is playing nicely and giving each other space. Sounds like chaos!

That's what roads were like when cars were first invented. They were clogged with horses, cars, streetcars, merchants and children. Countries tried different ways of controlling the traffic. In North America, laws had vehicles drive on the right, while in Britain, people had to drive on the left. Cities also experimented with traffic lights. The first traffic light in the world was installed in Britain in 1868. Unfortunately, it was a gas lamp, and it exploded.

For decades in North America, traffic lights were handheld. A police officer stood in the middle of the intersection, spinning a sign that said *stop* and *go*. It wasn't exactly safe, but at the time there was no other way.

GREEN MEANS GO

In 1914 a new system was tried in Cleveland. A police officer sat in a raised booth on the sidewalk, using an electric signal to control traffic. For the first time, drivers stopped at a traffic light. Red meant stop, and green meant go. Yellow, for slow down, was added in 1919 in Detroit, and it became standard. Crowds gathered at intersections to watch. Early on, an officer was there in case anything went wrong—and to explain the system to anyone who was confused.

Other changes began to happen at the same time. Trees were cut and grassy fields disappeared to widen roads and make space for sidewalks. Soon people started talking about making cars safer too. Can you guess what safety features were discussed?

Before there were automated traffic lights, signals were handheld. A police officer in Toronto directs traffic in this picture taken around 1920.
CITY OF TORONTO ARCHIVES, FONDS 1244, ITEM 1008

Horns and double headlamps—seat belts weren't invented until 1959!

More technology was invented to manage traffic. Toronto made history in 1963 by becoming the first city in the world to use a computerized traffic-management system. Today all traffic signals are managed in high-tech control centers. Computers keep track of traffic and make sure cars are moving. Technology has advanced traffic in a lot of ways, but one thing is the same: police are still around to help when the lights go out!

GETTING NOWHERE FAST

You've likely heard the words *rush hour* and **gridlock.** Rush hour is when lots of cars are driving at the same time, and gridlock is when traffic is blocked in all directions. They both mean it can take a long time to get from one place to another. It's very frustrating—just ask my son!

Let's look at how traffic jams begin. Imagine you have a group of people who all want to get through a doorway at the same time. The doorway seemed big enough when two people wanted to pass, but when you have 10, 100 or 1,000 people using the door at the same time, suddenly there's a lot less space. Now imagine one person crashes into another person and they

Buckle up—it's the law. Seat belts became mandatory in new cars in the United States in 1968. Since 1976 they have been required in Canada too.
KATE_SEPT2004/GETTY IMAGES

Congestion in cities around the world can bring vehicles to a standstill. This is a traffic jam in Shanghai.
BERNIE DECHANT/GETTY IMAGES

both fall down, blocking the doorway. Suddenly everyone is stuck. A bigger line forms, and people at the back have to wait longer even after the doorway is clear. By the 1970s, that's what was starting to happen in major cities around the world. The term *gridlock* was first used to describe traffic in New York City when the cars, buses and trucks on roads became "locked" in all directions on the "grid."

If there's one thing people can agree on, it's that nobody likes to travel in rush hour. The term *rush hour* is actually an oxymoron—the two words don't exactly go together! In some cities, like Toronto, Los Angeles, New York and London, rush hour is from 6 a.m. to 9 a.m. and from 3 p.m. to 7 p.m. In other cities, such as Delhi and Mumbai, India; Dhaka, Bangladesh; and Kampala, Uganda, to name a few, the whole day is an unending traffic nightmare, with cows in the roads along with rickshaws, double-decker buses and families piled on motorbikes.

STUCK IN TRAFFIC

Some cities have terrible traffic congestion. A company called INRIX calculated how many hours a year people spend stuck in gridlock. At the time I was writing this book, the top 10 most congested cities in the world were...

1. Bogotá, Colombia, 191 hours a year
2. Rio de Janeiro, Brazil, 190 hours a year
3. Mexico City, Mexico, 158 hours a year
4. Istanbul, Turkey, 153 hours a year
5. São Paulo, Brazil, 152 hours a year
6. Rome, Italy, 166 hours a year
7. Paris, France, 165 hours a year
8. London, England, 149 hours a year
9. Boston, United States, 149 hours a year
10. Chicago, United States, 145 hours a year

Just a typical rush hour in downtown Rio de Janeiro. Commuters spend a lot of time in traffic in this busy city.
LUOMAN/GETTY IMAGES

A young boy in Beijing wears a mask to protect his lungs from smog. In some countries the air is so polluted that people wear masks when they leave their homes.

HUNG_CHUNG_CHIH/GETTY IMAGES

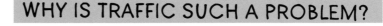

WHY IS TRAFFIC SUCH A PROBLEM?

It's hard to play games like cricket when the air is hazy with smog. This picture shows what it looks like in Kolkata, India.

DINODIA PHOTO/GETTY IMAGES

As we know, today there are more than a billion cars on the world's roads. If you lined up all those cars, they would wrap around Earth more than 150 times! By 2050, the number of cars will double to two billion. Most forms of transportation—cars, SUVs, vans, trucks, ships and airplanes—run on liquid fossil fuels such as gasoline or similar fuels. When an engine burns gas to make a vehicle move, it releases chemicals into the air, called *pollution*.

Cars and gas have become cleaner over the years. And, of course, cars aren't the only source of pollution. But with so many vehicles going farther and faster, and getting bigger, cars are a big part of the problem. In cities around the world, including Bishkek, Kyrgyzstan; Dhaka, Bangladesh; and Shenyang, China—the three most polluted cities—the air is so **toxic** that people have to wear face masks to get to work. Kids can't play outside without getting sick.

In some places, like the United States, Canada and the European Union, transportation is responsible for emitting up to 30 percent of all **carbon dioxide**, a greenhouse gas that heats the planet and leads to global warming. Transportation also contributes more than half of the **nitrogen oxides** in the air, toxins that make it hard for your lungs to work properly. Luckily, all over the world some pretty cool things are being done to manage traffic and shrink the number of cars on the road.

Which vehicles are the biggest polluters?

(Canada, 2018)

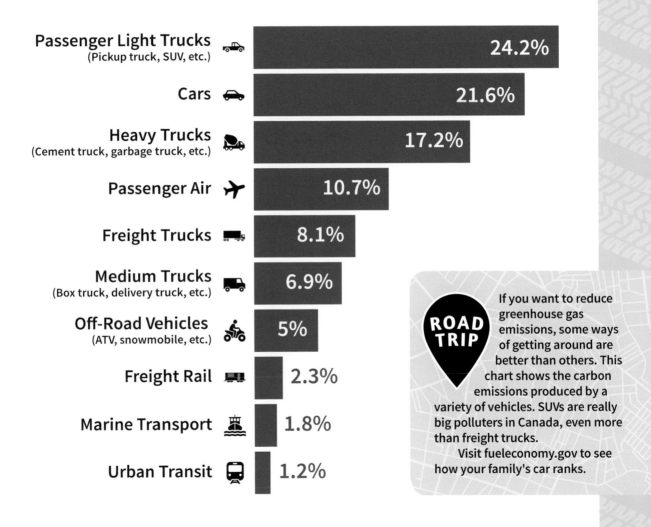

Passenger Light Trucks
(Pickup truck, SUV, etc.)   24.2%

Cars   21.6%

Heavy Trucks
(Cement truck, garbage truck, etc.)   17.2%

Passenger Air   10.7%

Freight Trucks   8.1%

Medium Trucks
(Box truck, delivery truck, etc.)   6.9%

Off-Road Vehicles
(ATV, snowmobile, etc.)   5%

Freight Rail   2.3%

Marine Transport   1.8%

Urban Transit   1.2%

ROAD TRIP

If you want to reduce greenhouse gas emissions, some ways of getting around are better than others. This chart shows the carbon emissions produced by a variety of vehicles. SUVs are really big polluters in Canada, even more than freight trucks.

Visit fueleconomy.gov to see how your family's car ranks.

DATA ADAPTED FROM NATURAL RESOURCES CANADA, TRANSPORTATION SECTOR,
TABLE 8: GHG EMISSIONS BY TRANSPORTATION MODE

CHAPTER TWO

Go with the Flow

IDLING GETS YOU NOWHERE

Being stuck in traffic, waiting for a parking spot and ordering at a drive-through restaurant have something in common. They all mean your car is idling, which is when it burns fuel but isn't moving. Millions of cars and trucks idle every day. It's bad for the planet and our health. Every gallon of gas burned produces almost 20 pounds of carbon dioxide (one liter produces 2.3 kilograms). That really adds up—the longer your car is running, the more emissions you produce. An easy way to help the planet is to remind your driver to turn off the car engine if you're going to be stopped for more than a minute. After all, idling literally gets you nowhere!

WAYS TO KEEP TRAFFIC MOVING

Experts are also tackling traffic in all sorts of ways. Some focus on helping traffic flow better so cars spend less time stuck on the road, while others are looking for ways to convince people not to drive at all. If you were in charge of traffic where you live, which of these strategies do you think would convince people to drive less?

Signs posted at school drop-off zones remind drivers to turn off their engines.
RICHARD JOHNSON/GETTY IMAGES

This is a high-tech traffic-control center in Scottsdale, AZ. Look at all the cameras monitoring traffic conditions in the city.

COURTESY OF SAMUEL KELLY, CITY OF SCOTTSDALE, AZ

THAT'S SMART! INTELLIGENT TRANSPORTATION SYSTEMS

Lots of cities around the world have high-tech traffic-control centers—brains—that manage everything from traffic signals and red-light cameras to the signs above our expressways. These are called *intelligent transportation systems*. They are part of what are called *smart cities*—places that use sensors, data and cameras to be "greener," safer and more efficient.

Smart cities have different ways of sensing traffic. There are loop detectors, video detection cameras, radar sensors and thermal detection cameras. Loop detectors are in the pavement and can feel when cars are waiting. The other sensors and cameras are higher up, on signal poles. When there are a lot of cars, sensors can change red lights to green to keep cars moving. Traffic engineers work behind the scenes to monitor these cameras.

IN THE DRIVER'S SEAT: An interview with a traffic engineer

Hong Huo is principal traffic engineer in Scottsdale, AZ—one of the best driving cities in America. Hong helps manage an intelligent transportation system that has over 300 traffic-signal systems, 175 miles (281 kilometers) of fiber-optic cable, more than 90 wireless radios and 170 pan-tilt-zoom cameras. This technology helps Hong and her team monitor traffic conditions and keep cars moving. It's an important job.

Q: What does a traffic engineer do?
A: Traffic engineers plan, design and operate traffic-control devices on roadways to make sure traffic flows safely and smoothly. These include signs, pavement markings, traffic signals and streetlighting. We do traffic studies, analyze traffic safety, identify high-crash locations and develop countermeasures to reduce crashes. We also handle the design of parking, cycling and pedestrian infrastructure.

Q: What do you love about your job?
A: I enjoy planning and designing creative solutions to keep traffic moving efficiently and safely. I like having a positive impact on people's daily lives.

Q: How did you become a traffic engineer?
A: I have degrees in civil engineering and systems and industrial engineering.

Q: How will technology help in the future?
A: Recent advances in sensor technology will provide more accurate and high-resolution data to improve traffic efficiency. More connectivity from connected-car and smart-car technology is expected to create a safer driving environment. Technologies that enable more people to work from home will also help reduce traffic congestion.

They can control traffic signals to tell drivers if there's an accident. They can also send police or ambulances to help, while tow trucks are radioed to move broken-down cars to the side of the road. Some cities can even tell drivers if there's congestion and reroute cars in real time. When a city is really smart, buses and cars will flow smoothly, get people where they need to go faster and produce fewer emissions in the process.

ALTERNATE DRIVING DAYS

In 1992 the United Nations named Mexico City the most polluted city on the planet. The Mexican government had to find ways to clean up the air. One of them is a program called *Hoy No Circula (No-Driving Day)*. Cars are not allowed on the road on certain days, based on their license-plate numbers.

Today Mexico City is no longer ranked as the most polluted city, but it wasn't just the no-driving days that helped. Improving public transportation, increasing bike-share programs and banning diesel cars, which emit dangerous pollutants, have all contributed. The use of driving restrictions is common in other cities too, such as São Paulo, Brazil; Quito, Ecuador; and Buenos Aires, Argentina. Experts hope these restrictions will help people change their transportation habits to curb pollution and traffic congestion.

Traffic barely moves on Paseo de la Reforma, a main road in downtown Mexico City.
NATE HOVEE/GETTY IMAGES

CONGESTION TAXES

London and Stockholm charge a fee, called a **congestion tax**, to drive into the city during busy times. This reduces traffic and pollution and encourages people to take public transit, **carpool** or drive in off-peak hours. People didn't like paying at first, but now most folks support the tax. The benefits are clear. One study looked at air pollution and asthma attacks in children in central Stockholm. Researchers compared data from before and after the tax's introduction in 2007. They found that pollution from cars decreased by 15 to 20 percent thanks to the tax. In addition, the number of children hospitalized from serious asthma attacks fell by 50 percent. Now more countries and cities are looking at using the same kinds of fees to decrease pollution and traffic.

Charging vehicles a toll to enter the city center really cuts down on traffic in areas that tend to get clogged with vehicles.
OLLO/GETTY IMAGES

LOW-EMISSION ZONES

If you want to drive in a **low-emission zone (LEZ)**, you'll need a car that meets low-emission standards. Alternative-fuel, **hybrid** or **zero-emission vehicles** are welcome, but gas-powered cars are discouraged. Drivers who enter an LEZ and don't meet the standard have to pay a fee, or they will be fined. The city of London, England, has tough new LEZ rules. Anyone who breaks them will be fined up to 500 pounds (about 680 US dollars). This strategy is meant to reduce air pollution and encourage walking, cycling, public transportation and electric cars. The zones will cut nitrogen oxide emissions by 84 percent, clearing the air for thousands of schoolchildren in these zones. Many countries in Europe, including Germany, Belgium, Denmark, Greece and the Netherlands, have LEZs, and Japan, Singapore and China do too. Many experts say that creating LEZs is the best way to improve air quality in towns and cities.

In cities such as London, UK (pictured), signs like these discourage drivers of gas-powered vehicles from entering certain areas. It's an effective way to keep the air clean.
DANIEL BEREHULAK/GETTY IMAGES

London is so serious about reducing air pollution that it even introduced ultra-low-emission zones (ULEZs) across the city in 2019. Harmful emissions there dropped five times as fast as they did in the rest of the United Kingdom.

LIFE IS A HIGHWAY

There are ways to get traffic moving better on highways. Ramp meters are traffic signals that make cars merge onto the highway one at a time. When highways are jam-packed with traffic, some cities open a "part-time shoulder" for cars or buses, which widens the highway. There are also variable speed limits—electronic signs that lower the speed limit on parts of the highway when there is heavy traffic or bad weather. All of these strategies reduce congestion and accidents.

Many highway entry ramps have a signal that helps cars merge onto the highway one at a time. This one is in Auckland.

CAR-SHARING PROGRAMS

According to the British Parking Association, drivers in the United Kingdom spend nearly four days a year looking for parking. When a driver finds a spot, another thing happens—the car sits there all day. The average car is parked more than 90 percent of the time and carries only one person when it's in motion. *Car- and ride-sharing* services like Uber, Lyft and ZipCar decrease the number of cars on the road, reduce the need for parking and increase the use of other forms of transportation. One ride-sharing company, BlaBlaCar, has kept more than 1.8 million tons (1.6 million tonnes) of carbon dioxide out of the atmosphere. The company began offering rides in France and has now expanded to 22 countries, from Spain and Serbia to Russia and Romania. Some car-sharing companies even specialize in sharing *electric vehicles*, which means they produce zero emissions. Imagine how great it would be if all those unneeded parking lots could be used for other things, like green space, playgrounds or bike paths.

Car-sharing is a great way to reduce traffic, especially since many vehicles are parked for much of the day.

CARPOOLING

Carpooling is another great way to share rides and cut the number of cars on the road. High-occupancy vehicle (HOV) lanes are reserved for cars with more than one person inside. These special lanes have been used in the United States and Canada for decades, and the concept has expanded to China, Europe and Australia. Reserved lanes get carpoolers to work faster than if each person drove their own car. Carpooling is also a great way to reduce congestion and pollution. Many companies are doing a great job of encouraging people to drive to work together.

Carpooling makes sense, and it's fun too!
JGI/JAMIE GRILL/GETTY IMAGES

ROAD TRIP

When Nike moved its headquarters to Beaverton, OR, in 1992, 98 percent of employees drove to work alone. Nike management wanted to change that. They wanted employees to be healthier and less stressed when they arrived at work, and they wanted them to contribute to caring for the environment. To encourage people to find better ways to get to work, they offer incentives to employees who carpool, bike or use public transportation. They match carpoolers and offer them better parking spots. They hand out free public-transit passes, and a Nike shuttle takes employees from the train station to work. A bike-sharing program lets staff ride around campus for free during the day. Onsite services such as childcare, dry cleaning, grocery stores, a beauty salon and fitness centers mean people don't need their car during the day. The effort has worked. The number of people who drove to work alone dropped by 26 percent within a few years of launching the program. Thanks to its environmental leadership, Nike has been named one of the Environmental Protection Agency's Best Workplaces for Commuters.

At Nike headquarters, employees are encouraged to find healthy ways to get to work.
VDB PHOTOS/SHUTTERSTOCK.COM

This bike is extra helpful—especially if you're riding home with your Christmas tree!

ROAD TRIP

The Danes are known for many things, including the Danish pastry, Vikings, the invention of Lego and being the happiest people in the world. They are also famous for their love of cycling—and a bold goal. They want Copenhagen to become the world's first *carbon-neutral* capital city by 2025.

- 62 percent of people in the city ride a bike to get to work or school each day—that's more people biking in a day than in the entire United States.

- There are five times more bicycles than cars in the city center—only 14 percent of people drive a car every day.

- Together, cyclists in Copenhagen bike 0.75 million miles (1.2 million kilometers) every day. Bicycle Super Highways—wide, safe, high-speed bicycle lanes—connect dozens of towns to the city center.

- Garbage bins are angled diagonally so cyclists can easily toss their trash. There are even footrests at traffic lights so cyclists don't have to get off their bikes while they wait.

BORROW A BIKE

Many people are realizing they don't need their own car—and they don't even need their own bike. They can borrow a bike when they need one and drop it off when they're done. Bike-sharing programs are popular all over the world. According to one estimate, there are more than 1,600 bike-sharing programs in over 1,200 cities around the world. That adds up to more than 18 million shared bicycles. Hangzhou, China, has the biggest bike-sharing program. At last count it had 86,000 bikes and 473,000 daily rides. Vancouver, British Columbia, also has a program that "uses its head"—every rental comes with a helmet. In some cities, like Tel Aviv, Israel, you can even borrow an electric scooter.

Bike-sharing is popular in cities around the world. These bikes can be rented in Melbourne.

20-MINUTE NEIGHBORHOODS

In many cities, zoning laws make it illegal to live near businesses and stores. These laws were created decades ago so people wouldn't have to smell pollution from factories or live near restaurant garbage containers. Now many cities are changing how space is used. They're updating zoning laws and creating complete communities, or **20-minute neighborhoods**, where people can shop, eat, go to the library, play at the park or visit the dentist within a short, safe walk from home.

Melbourne is one of Australia's fastest-growing cities. The population is currently over 5 million people, but this could increase to 8.5 million by 2050. To ensure the city can support so many people, a series of 20-minute neighborhoods is being tested. The hope is that within the next 35 years, Melbourne will be transformed into a series of vibrant, livable neighborhoods in which people can live, work and play within a 20-minute walk from home. Each will be sustainable, with plenty of safe cycling and public transportation options too. The plan is ambitious, but other cities, such as Singapore, are looking to Melbourne as a leader. Which city inspired Melbourne? Experts say Portland, Oregon, was first to champion 20-minute neighborhoods. It's already ahead of the pack—by 2030, 90 percent of Portlandians will be able to walk or cycle easily to wherever they need to go within 20 minutes of leaving home.

Portland, OR, is a very livable city. It was the first to champion the 20-minute neighborhood concept, which means everything you need is within walking distance.
PORTLAND EDIBLE GARDENS

Pedestrians, not cars, fill open spaces in Times Square, New York City.
ANDRE BENZ/UNSPLASH.COM

RECLAIMING THE STREETS

Hundreds of cities are closing off streets to traffic. Times Square in New York City is a car-free zone with chairs that invite people to sit and hang out. Paris banned traffic along part of the Seine River. There were once 40,000 cars cutting through the city. Now, instead of lanes for cars, there are open spaces for people to walk or picnic.

This car-free Sunday in Jakarta, Indonesia, attracts big crowds.

© DIDIER MARTI/GETTY IMAGES

Many other cities around the world are also ***reclaiming the streets***—even temporarily. On Sundays, about two million people in Bogotá, Colombia, enjoy *Ciclovía*, the biggest recreation event in the world. Just imagine—it's a typical Sunday in Bogotá, and the sun is shining. You head toward a main street and find yourself surrounded by people cycling, walking, dancing, roller-blading and skateboarding. You hear music in the park, and your stomach rumbles as you pass a street vendor selling arepas. You have plenty of time to enjoy the fun, since more than 74 miles (120 kilometers) of roads are blocked off to car traffic from 7 a.m. until 2 p.m. Ciclovía is so fun that about 30 percent of residents show up every week. The event has inspired more than 400 other cities to have their own car-free days. Even cities as far away as Addis Ababa, Ethiopia, have "open street" days when people can safely dance, skateboard and play soccer in the streets without having to worry about cars.

CAR-FREE NEIGHBORHOODS

Can you imagine a neighborhood without cars? ***Superblocks*** are a reality in Barcelona, where traffic is routed *around* neighborhoods, not through them. Superblocks consist of neighborhoods of nine blocks that are reserved for cycling and walking and other car-free activities. Only emergency and delivery vehicles are allowed in. Even then, lanes have been narrowed, the speed limit has been reduced and pedestrians have the right-of-way. A handful of these superblocks have been created since 2016, but there are plans to convert the entire city. There are proposals to change intersections to pedestrian plazas, plant trees and create more green space and more space for people to enjoy. Experts say it's one of the biggest changes to a major European city in this century. Mayor Ada Colau said to think of it as "the new city for the present and the future—with less pollution, new mobility and new public space."

When cars have to go around neighborhoods instead of through them, it's safer for kids to play—and for others to use bikes and scooters to get around.

SHIHAN SHAN/GETTY IMAGES

When cities are built vertically instead of being spread out, there's more room for things like parks.
3000AD/SHUTTERSTOCK.COM

CITIES OF THE FUTURE?

Instead of converting neighborhoods, China is designing its first car-free city from scratch. There are plans for the Great City to be built outside Chengdu. It's named Great City for a reason. Architects are designing the city around a transportation hub that will connect residents to other cities. Within the neighborhood, people will be able to walk wherever they need to go—and they'll get there within 15 minutes. Everything residents need will be packed closely together in tall buildings. That's because the city will be vertical, rather than spread out, to increase *density* (the number of people that can live in a space). The only thing people won't need is cars. How dense will it be? About 30,000 families, or 80,000 people, will move into a space that's just 0.5 square miles (1.3 square kilometers)—a bit bigger than a typical golf course.

A transportation hub like this will connect one car-free city to another. How convenient!
MAHLUM/WIKIMEDIA COMMONS/PUBLIC DOMAIN

New technology and simple ideas are making people rethink what cities are, how to improve them and what they should look like in the years ahead. But what about those flying cars? Let's move along to the future of transportation…

CHAPTER THREE

Driving into the Future

C ars won't have wings anytime soon, but talking cars and cars that can drive themselves are in the works. And soon you may even be able to ride in a train that goes as fast as a plane.

CARS THAT DRIVE THEMSELVES

In the future, cars may not need a human behind the wheel—self-driving cars will be operated by computers. They are being tested now for safety and aren't fully approved for driving on main roads. Experts think this technology will one day make driving safer and reduce accidents. That's because computers are programmed to drive at the perfect speed and keep the best distance from other cars around them. Plus, they don't get distracted, fall asleep at the wheel or have road rage.

WHY AREN'T SELF-DRIVING CARS ALREADY ON ROADS?

Nobody knows when we will have self-driving cars, says Dr. Lina Kattan, an expert in transportation and technology at the University of Calgary. "They have to prove to be very safe, better than human driving," she explains.

Dr. Lina Kattan researches transportation and technology in her lab at the University of Calgary.
COURTESY OF DR. LINA KATTAN

One day you might be able to get behind the wheel of a self-driving car and read a book while you commute! This is what the driver's seat might look like by the time you get your license.
METAMORWORKS/SHUTTERSTOCK.COM

Cars that drive themselves have other benefits besides safety. "We'll be able to send our cars home alone so we don't need parking lots," Kattan says. But this could also create challenges. "If too many people [were to] send their cars home alone to avoid paying for parking, we might have more traffic and thus more congestion."

There are still a lot of issues to discuss. Legal experts are debating who's responsible if there's an accident. Would it be the car manufacturer, the person who owns the car or the company that made the software for the car? What happens if there's a computer malfunction and something goes wrong? What about threats from cyberattacks?

Finally, what happens when there are both human-driven and computer-driven cars on the roads? Dr. Kattan thinks self-driving cars will set a good example for the rest of us.

Cars are getting more high-tech. Here's a rear-view camera, a feature that is now required in new cars in Canada.
RYOSHA/GETTY IMAGES

27

"Humans can make mistakes," she says, adding that frequent lane changes can cause accidents. "When you have self-driving cars, they are programmed to behave. On busy roads and when there are [many self-driving cars], people will have to follow cars in front. [The self-driving cars] will act like role models on busy roads."

As the technology continues to evolve, Dr. Kattan has some advice that always applies. "Be more active. Try to leave the car at home and take transit, walk and bike as a healthier habit."

'TALKING' CARS

Drivers will also be able to own "connected cars"—that is, cars that can talk to traffic signals and other cars. When cars are able to coordinate with one another, traffic will flow more easily. Cars will also help each other avoid accidents. If there's black ice or a stopped car on the road ahead, one car can alert the others. Cars don't have these abilities yet, but talking-car technology is being tested.

One day in the not-too-distant future, cars will be able to communicate with each other.
POSTERIORI/SHUTTERSTOCK.COM

HIGH-TECH PUBLIC TRANSPORTATION

When public transportation is faster and more convenient than driving, people will leave their cars at home. That's why experts are working to make buses better. One day we could end up with self-driving buses, buses that can talk to each other and buses that can communicate with traffic signals to create priority bus lanes during rush hour. There could even be buses that can call for backup when crowds of people are waiting.

Singapore is testing these high-tech solutions. The city is using self-driving buses and on-demand shuttles so people who live far from a bus stop can order a shuttle on their phone and it will bring them to a transportation hub where they can catch a bus or subway. Until all cities have shuttles like these, personal apps like Moovit, Citymapper and Transit are already helping millions of people get around faster using public transportation. These apps can do cool things, such as map out the best way to get people where they need to go, based on real-time information.

ELECTRIC BUSES

Many cities are phasing out old buses and rolling out new hybrid, hydrogen-powered or zero-emission electric buses. Shenzhen, China, is one of just a few cities to have an entire fleet of electric buses. London, England, has converted all of its double-decker buses to meet low-emission standards. Along with the LEZs mentioned earlier, this change is expected to reduce nitrogen oxide emissions by 84 percent in those LEZs. By 2037, all of London's roughly 9,200 buses will be zero-emission.

But it seems China is leading the way. At last count the world had about 425,000 electric buses, about 99 percent of them (421,000) in China.

Even rail transport is becoming more climate-friendly. Germany has bought hybrid electric trains that can run on overhead power lines. They are expected to be running by 2024.

PIT STOP
It's going to take a long time for the rest of the world to have as many zero-emission e-buses on the road as China does. But progress is being made. In 2019, Europe had 2,250 electric buses. The United States had about 300, and though that doesn't sound like many, this was a 32 percent jump from the previous year.

On the left is an electric car from 1896. Yes, some of the first cars ever driven were electric. Compare that to a new Tesla (right). This one is filling up at an electric charging station.
LEFT: HULTON ARCHIVE/GETTY IMAGES; RIGHT: SEAN GALLUP/GETTY IMAGES

ELECTRIC VEHICLES

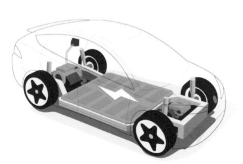

A Tesla has way fewer parts than a typical car. The base looks like a skateboard!
PETOVARGA/SHUTTERSTOCK.COM

You might be surprised to learn that the first cars invented were electric. In fact, at the turn of the last century, from about 1900 to 1912, one of every three cars on US roads was battery-powered. Today electric cars look very different, and they're more popular too. There are even superfast charging stations so people with electric vehicles (EVs) can power up at a mall or office faster than you can charge a cell phone.

EVs have very heavy batteries. They can weigh as much as 1,500 pounds (680 kilograms)—about the weight of a cow! If you flipped a Tesla on its back, it would look more like a skateboard than a car. That's because electric cars don't have engines or many parts. You plug the car into the wall to charge it, like any other electronic device. The car uses the electricity from the battery to spin its wheels. It produces zero emissions and almost no sound while you're driving. Compare that to typical cars that have internal combustion engines and run on gas. They are noisy, create pollution and have over 200 parts.

There are other types of low-emission cars too. You might have heard of hybrid cars that run on gas and battery charge, and cars that run on hydrogen or liquid natural gas, which means

they produce little to no emissions. Car companies are also working on cars that run on biofuels such as plant oils. Your car might already run on corn. That's because a percentage of gasoline comes from ethanol, or corn alcohol, which is a cleaner form of gas. Over the last several decades, governments have been making cars and gas cleaner, but experts say electric cars will be the cleanest and most common option for the future. Many countries and car manufacturers are planning to make most or all new cars electric within the next 20 years.

This Tesla Model S accelerates faster than a race car. I took a test drive in one, and it made my stomach lurch!
ABU HASIM.A/SHUTTERSTOCK.COM

IT'S A BIRD, IT'S A PLANE, IT'S A HYPERLOOP TRAIN!

There's been a lot of excitement about a new kind of train called the **hyperloop**, which will one day be able to take passengers from one major city to another in minutes rather than hours. That means you could live in Los Angeles and be at work in San Francisco in 50 minutes. It would take half a day to drive there by car. Hyperloop train technology combines magnetic levitation (the train floats above the track) with a vacuum-sealed tube (which removes air resistance) and uses little energy to travel at speeds of up to 670 mph (1,078 km/h). A hyperloop train costs more than $6 billion to build, so it may be a while before one pulls into a train station near you.

ROAD TRIP Some Teslas are superfast. The Tesla Model S can accelerate faster than any sports car in a race—even if the Tesla carried a family of five and their luggage. It goes from 0 to 60 mph (0 to 100 km/h) in two seconds. The Bugatti Chiron mentioned in chapter 1 would take 2.5 seconds—plus it's very expensive and only seats two people. Electric cars can accelerate faster than gas-powered cars partly because power is provided instantly by electricity, so the wheels can start turning right away. Picture a drill—you pull the trigger, and it starts to spin right away. An internal combustion engine takes four separate steps to generate power. This means that the fastest race cars can overtake a Tesla, but only once their engines have started.

The hyperloop train is superfast. There are lots of videos online that explain how it works.
ANDREY_I/SHUTTERSTOCK.COM

Olli shuttles are made using 3D printers and materials that can be recycled.
LEFT: MIKEDOTTA/SHUTTERSTOCK.COM; RIGHT: WESTEND61/GETTY IMAGES

IN THE DRIVER'S SEAT: Local Motors reimagines the future of transportation

Local Motors is a small company with big dreams. With a microfactory in Tennessee and its offices in Arizona, this company uses only the materials it needs to build green transportation solutions. It created the world's first 3D-printed car and the first 3D-printed autonomous electric vehicle, named Olli. I spoke to Johnny Scotello at Local Motors to find out more.

Q: What is Olli?
A: Olli is a 3D-printed electric zero-emission vehicle. It's a self-driving vehicle that can take me from my house to the train station. Or it might pick up kids from the neighborhood and take them to school. It can transport eight people at once and is a great option for cities, hospitals, campuses, stadiums and parks.

Q: How is it different from a school bus?
A: Unlike a school bus, Olli doesn't produce emissions. Olli can also drive itself. Currently a safety attendant is there to supervise, but eventually they won't be needed. Olli is also much smaller than a bus, and in the future riders will be able to call it on demand. This means that a student could use a smartphone to call Olli to their stop. Students would spend less time waiting for the bus to arrive, and Olli automatically skips stops where there are no kids waiting.

Q: How does Local Motors make vehicles in an environmentally friendly way?
A: We make Olli at a microfactory. When you use a smaller space, you consume less energy. We customize each vehicle and only produce the number we need. Our 3D printer uses recycled material and prints just the parts we need, with very little waste. Also, because the parts are printed out of composite, when an Olli reaches the end of its life, it can be ground down and used to make another Olli. That means less of the vehicle ends up in a landfill.

Q: What do you think driving will be like in the future?
A: Some people will always own personal vehicles, but we can make shared transportation that's good for the planet and useful for everyone. Lots of companies are working on self-driving vehicles. This technology can change how we live and how our cities are designed. If we need to get somewhere, most people will use shared transportation. This way we spend less time looking for a parking spot. Parking lots, garages and driveways can become green space for everyone.

Q: How can kids make a difference?
A: Kids can make a difference by understanding that emissions are not good for the planet. Taking the bus, riding a bike and walking are great choices to decrease emissions and waste. The other way to contribute is to work hard in school so that someday you too can help make technologies like Olli a reality. We need scientists and engineers to research and develop new technologies. We need businesspeople to figure out how to design, build and sell them. And we need lawmakers to make laws and policies that encourage companies to put environmentally friendly vehicles on the road. With a great education, you could be that person who helps make a difference.

TRAFFIC DISAPPEARS

When the COVID-19 pandemic began to spread around the world in March 2020, traffic came to a halt. Literally. All around the world, people were ordered to stay inside. Schools, offices, stores and even parks were closed, and people were told not to leave their houses unless they needed to get groceries or pick up medicine, or they had a medical emergency. Traffic decreased instantly. In London, England, traffic was down 60 percent in the first five weeks of the lockdown, as was air pollution. With no boats or water taxis, the canals in Venice became so clear that people could see fish in the water for the first time in recent memory. In northern India, people were able to see the Himalayas for the first time in decades.

An opportunity for change

The city of Milan, one of the most polluted and congested in Europe, is taking advantage of the "once-in-a-lifetime" opportunity created by the pandemic. When the city went into lockdown, traffic congestion dropped 30 to 75 percent, along with air pollution. Officials want to keep cars from clogging the roads for good. But how? Before the pandemic, 55 percent of the population relied on public transportation. Now, with everyone worried about their health, those commuters might decide they're safer in a car. To prevent that from happening, Milan is making changes in advance. The city is expanding space for cyclists and walkers, reducing the speed limit on streets and making active transportation the priority. They're hoping the pandemic can be a way to change people's habits and keep congestion and pollution down in the long term. It's being called one of the most ambitious plans in Europe, and other cities are looking to Milan as an example.

One thing the pandemic showed...

Remember those employees at Nike headquarters? During the pandemic, most of them worked from home. And they did a good job too. In fact, the pandemic proved to many companies that employees can be just as productive working from home as in the office. If people are allowed to work from home, or are asked to come to work on alternating days, traffic and pollution might stay low. Rush hour might even disappear. On the other hand, if people return to work, traffic could increase if they decide they feel more comfortable driving personal vehicles instead.

ROAD TRIP A company called TomTom measures traffic patterns all over the world. In 2020 it saw a huge decrease in traffic, unlike anything seen before. What did the team find?

- Traffic decreased in 387 cities.
- Some cities had as many as 30 days of low traffic, with congestion half of what it was on the same day in 2019.
- Minneapolis had the most days of low traffic—219—with congestion levels at least 50 percent lower than on the same day in 2019.
- In Paris on October 29, 2020, the day before new lockdowns were introduced, many people tried to escape the city at the same time. Traffic jams reached record lengths. By 6 p.m. congestion levels in Paris hit 142 percent.

Traffic disappeared in Milan and in many cities around the world during the first COVID-19 lockdown in March 2020.
EUGENIO MARONGIU/GETTY IMAGES

How Kids Can Help Drive Change

You can't drive. In fact, you're still years away from getting your license. Yet all over the world, kids like you are reducing traffic and helping the planet by finding more active ways to get from place to place. They are changing their habits and influencing the way adults use transportation.

HAND OUT PARKING TICKETS

Pollution from cars is worse in places where idling is common, such as near schools. Many schools have a no-idling policy, but drivers of cars and buses don't always follow the rules. Kids are taking action to help the planet—and each other. After a rise in asthma cases at an elementary school in Greater Manchester, students gave out fake parking tickets to parents in idling cars. This reminded drivers to turn off their engines in school zones. There are many other ways kids are helping educate people about the dangers of idling. They are talking about it on the morning announcements, making posters to hang on the walls and enforcing no-idling zones outside their schools.

Handing out fake parking tickets to idling drivers is a great way to remind people to turn off their engines.
ANDS456/GETTY IMAGES

Kids in London, UK, wore special backpacks that measured air quality on their routes to school. They helped scientists discover better ways for students to get to school.
JAMES JIAO/SHUTTERSTOCK.COM

BECOME RESEARCH ASSISTANTS

In spring 2019, more than 250 students participated in a study to monitor air quality in London, England. Children from five different primary schools wore backpacks with state-of-the-art air-quality sensors on their way to school and in the classroom. The results showed that air pollution was five times higher on the way to school than when they were in the classroom. They also found that children who walked along main roads were exposed to the highest levels of pollution, while kids taking side streets had less exposure. Thanks to the work of these young air-quality scientists, changes were made so that students would be exposed to lower levels of pollution. At one of the schools that participated, students created a new green space at the corner of their school to help block pollution from a busy street nearby. Some children took different routes to school, such as walking on side streets instead of main roads. Schools prevented cars from getting close to school main entrances, and new rules were created and enforced to stop idling at pickup and drop-off points. The backpack study was such an exciting project that students were still talking about what they had learned, and thinking about what else they could do, long after the study was over.

Kids are taking steps to create a healthier future.
MAYUR KAKADE/GETTY IMAGES

Crossing guards make sure cars stop for kids going to and from school.
FATCAMERA/GETTY IMAGES

JOIN THE SAFETY PATROL

Across North America, student volunteers participate in their school's safety patrol program. Organizations such as the Canadian Automobile Association and the American Automobile Association provide stop signs, bright orange vests and training so that older students can help younger students cross streets safely on their way to school. If walking to school is safer for kids, parents don't have to drive them. Patrolling is a big job, and an important one too. Kids learn to watch for distracted drivers, make eye contact with drivers and look left-right-left again before and while crossing, even when kids have the right-of-way.

SPEAK UP TO MAKE STREETS SAFER

Josh Fullan's job was to help make streets safer for communities. He realized kids weren't involved in discussions, so he decided to change that. He founded a company called Maximum City. In one of his projects, Josh worked with students in sixth and seventh grade from the Sterling Hall School in Toronto. Over three years, students studied busy streets near their school. They concluded that the area wasn't safe for people walking, taking the bus or even shopping. Instead, the whole area was safest for drivers. The students brought the entire community together and worked with city staff and councilors to get the speed limit reduced. They also added a stop sign at an unsafe T intersection.

Other schools, from Toronto to Frankfurt, are also working with Maximum City to improve their neighborhoods. What makes streets safer for pedestrians? They can be designed with narrower roadways, traffic-calming bumps, signs, trees, protected bike lanes, wider sidewalks and pathways, and shorter crossings at busy intersections—anything that gives drivers a visual or physical cue to go slower.

Think about your neighborhood. Can you easily and safely walk to school? Do you feel comfortable riding a bike in your area? Find out how your neighborhood ranks by visiting maximumcity.ca/kidscore.

PIT STOP

Sidewalks have been around since ancient times. The first ones date back to Turkey in 2000 BCE. They've gone in and out of style over the centuries and look different in cities around the world. Today sidewalks are in fashion— and having good sidewalks encourages people to use them.

Maximum City worked with schools to develop a walking-tour curriculum and resource guide for students. Pictured here are kids participating in Jane's Walk School Edition. It's all about improving neighborhoods for pedestrians.
JOSH FULLAN

WALK TO SCHOOL

Kids everywhere are finding ways to make walking to school a regular activity. It's a great way to reduce traffic and pollution and get more exercise. Some kids join a *walking school bus*—a group of kids who walk to school together or with an adult. If your school doesn't have a walking school bus, you can start your own. Visit walkingschoolbus.org to learn how.

Lots of kids also participate in International Walk to School Month in October. In Victoria, Australia, 186,602 elementary schoolchildren walked, rode or scootered to school in October 2019—that was the highest number in the program's history and 25 percent more than in 2018.

Sure, Australia has good weather. But you can walk to school in winter too. In Ajax, Ontario, a student-led committee at Da Vinci Public School planned a Winter Walk Day in February. They handed out hot chocolate to walkers, along with inspirational notes encouraging kids to keep on going!

A walking school bus like this one gets kids walking together.
CAVAN IMAGES/GETTY IMAGES

ROAD TRIP

Annabelle Vestal from Fairhope, AL, was just five years old when she met her town's mayor on a school field trip. She asked him if he could build a sidewalk connecting her neighborhood to downtown Fairhope, so she and her friends could safely walk or bike to school and the park. It took years of bringing the mayor cookies, writing him notes, getting community members to sign a petition, monitoring traffic patterns and presenting her case to officials, but eventually the city council agreed. Annabelle was eight years old when construction began. To show her appreciation for the construction workers and politicians, she brought donuts and cookies to the construction site. Now she and her friends walk to school every day in a walking school bus.

Step this way! Annabelle Vestal walks on the sidewalk she petitioned for. Now everyone can use it.
COURTESY OF JENNIFER SAMETINI VESTAL

Maddie Popielak and her mom, Dee Scharff, worked hard with many others to make the Ruby Bridges Walk to School Day a success.
COURTESY OF PETER FENG

PLAN A SPECIAL EVENT

A fifth-grade class at Martin Elementary School in South San Francisco was inspired by the courage of Ruby Bridges, the first Black student to integrate an all-white school in the 1960s. Each day that Ruby walked to school, her entire community walked with her, showing their support as she braved insults and even violence from people who didn't want Black and white students to go to school together. Determined to honor her, the fifth-graders at Martin Elementary organized an annual Ruby Bridges Walk to School Day on November 14—Ruby's first day at school. A few hundred students participated in the first walk, in 2018. Now the event has expanded to schools across the United States. The students who organized the first event with their teacher eventually got to meet Ruby herself. The walk shows what a big impact kids can have when they work together for change.

Ruby Bridges played a major role in integrating American schools in the 1960s. The Ruby Bridges Walk honors her bravery.
UNCREDITED DOJ PHOTOGRAPHER/
WIKIMEDIA COMMONS/PUBLIC DOMAIN

Biking to school is a great way to get exercise. You'll also arrive more ready to learn.

WAVEBREAKMEDIA/GETTY IMAGES

BIKE TO SCHOOL

Similar to a walking school bus, a **bicycle train** is a group of kids (and sometimes adults too) who bike to school together. A group of girls from Seward Montessori in Minneapolis made headlines when they decided to bike to school every day for a whole school year, no matter the weather. They braved foggy glasses and deep snow, and inspired their entire school in the process. Before long more kids were riding to school. The community stepped up, offering riding lessons to new cyclists and organizing field trips. Parents helped fix bikes and change tires. Of course, big motivators were the waffles and hot chocolate on Fridays.

Bike Week events are another way for communities to try active transportation. These are usually held in May, leading up to World Bicycle Day on June 3. Walking and cycling are great ways to get exercise and cut down on driving. Why not start your own school event? Visit walkbiketoschool.org for ideas.

TAKE PUBLIC TRANSPORTATION OR CARPOOL

Public transportation helps reduce traffic and pollution. In many places, kids ride for free.

BLEND IMAGES - GRANGER WOOTZ/GETTY IMAGES

Sometimes it isn't possible to walk or bike to school. But instead of having someone drive only you, maybe you can carpool. Public buses are also great ways to get around. One full city bus equals more than 60 people driving alone. Plus, people who use trains and buses take 30 percent more steps per day than people who drive. In many cities, kids ride for free!

Taking the school bus also reduces traffic. One school bus takes about 36 cars off the road. When you add it all up, school buses keep more than 17 million cars from commuting each day in the United States. School districts are finding ways to cut back on traffic even more. The Toronto District School Board found that by having elementary schools start and end at different times, 55 fewer buses are needed, which keeps almost 3,306 tons (3,000 tonnes) of carbon dioxide from getting into the air each year. It's a simple solution with a big impact.

TELL IT LIKE IT IS

Do your parents let the car idle when your baby sibling naps in the car? Is the car kept running to listen to the radio or while you're eating a burger from a drive-through restaurant? Ask your adult to turn off the engine.

Talk to your parents about their driving habits. After reading this book, you might know some things they don't!
JGI/TOM GRILL/GETTY IMAGES

If you live in a cold city, like I do, you often see cars idling in the driveway to heat up. It turns out Canadians idle their vehicles in winter for more than 75 million minutes a day. That's like letting one car idle for 144 years. Remind your parent that the best way to warm up a car on a cold day is to drive it. They'll save gas and reduce pollution too. The same goes for cooling off your car in summer. By sharing information, you'll impress others with how much you know *and* help the environment.

Lots of people are in the habit of getting around by car. But kids can make a big difference to traffic when they choose to walk, cycle, carpool or take public transportation. They can also help others be mindful of their habits.

In fact, writing *Rush Hour* has had a big impact on my life. My family and I leave the car at home more often than we used to. We walk more, and when we need to go a bit farther, we get on our bikes. My kids have rollerblades too. These are all great forms of active transportation. It makes us feel healthier, more connected and like we're doing our part to reduce traffic and pollution.

Scootering takes practice, but it can be a great way to get around.
CAVAN IMAGES/GETTY IMAGES

I'm not going to change rush hour alone. I'm not going to clean the air by walking or biking a lot. But if we all do a little more, drive a little less, change some of our habits and see transportation in a new way, we'll make a difference together.

Resources

Apps

BBC Earth

National Geographic

WWF Together

Websites

calc.zerofootprint.net

climatekids.nasa.gov

davidsuzuki.org

epa.gov/carbon-footprint-calculator

epa.gov/greenvehicles/find-smartway-vehicle

fueleconomy.gov

inrix.com/scorecard

localmotors.com

maximumcity.ca/kidscore

saferoutespartnership.org

tomtom.com/en_gb/traffic-index

walkbiketoschool.org

walkingschoolbus.org

walkscore.com/cities-and-neighborhoods

Documentaries, TV Shows and Videos

A Beautiful Planet. Directed by Toni Myers. Narrated by Jennifer Lawrence. 2016; United States: IMAX, Walt Disney Studios/Netflix. Documentary.

David Attenborough: A Life on Our Planet. Directed by JonathanHughes, Alastair Fothergill and Keith Scholey. Narrated by David Attenborough. 2020; United States: Netflix. Documentary.

I Am Greta. Directed by Nathan Grossman. 2020; Germany: Hulu, Dogwoof. Documentary.

An Inconvenient Sequel: Truth To Power. Directed by Jon Shenk and Bonni Cohen. Screenplay by Al Gore. 2017; United States: Paramount Pictures. Documentary.

A Plastic Ocean. Directed by Craig Leeson. 2016; United States: Netflix. Documentary.

"Something in the Air." *The Nature of Things.* Directed by Leif Kaldor. February 17, 2019; Canada: CBC. Documentary.

"Watch the Hyperloop Complete Its First Successful Test Ride." *Wired.* July 12, 2017. https://www.youtube.com/watch?v=O_FyOBCVGWE

Books

Clinton, Chelsea. *It's Your World: Get Informed, Get Inspired & Get Going!* New York: Philomel Books, 2015.

Clinton, Chelsea. *Start Now! You Can Make a Difference.* New York: Philomel Books, 2018.

Gore, Al. *Our Choice: How We Can Solve the Climate Crisis* (Young Reader Edition). New York: Puffin Books, 2009.

Green, Jen. *50 Things You Should Know about the Environment.* London: QED Publishing Inc., 2016.

Herman, Gail. *What Is Climate Change?* New York: Penguin, 2018.

Ignotofsky, Rachel. *The Wondrous Workings of Planet Earth: Understanding Our World and Its Ecosystems.* Berkeley, CA: Ten Speed Press, 2018.

Magoon, Kekla, and Chelsea Clinton. *She Persisted: Ruby Bridges.* New York: Philomel Books, 2021.

Mulder, Michelle. *Brilliant! Shining a Light on Sustainable Energy.* Victoria, BC: Orca Book Publishers, 2016.

Reynolds, Eddie. *Climate Crisis for Beginners.* London: Usborne Books, 2021.

Glossary

20-minute neighborhoods—"complete neighborhoods" where people can shop, eat, go to the library, play at the park, visit the dentist and so on within a short, safe walk from home

assembly line—a way of manufacturing in which things are built or assembled in a specific order to improve speed and efficiency. The concept revolutionized the way everything from cars to McDonald's hamburgers are made.

bicycle train—a group of kids (and adults) who bike to school together

carbon dioxide—a heat-trapping greenhouse gas released through deforestation and burning fossil fuels, for example. When there is too much, it causes Earth's temperature to rise, called *global warming*. This leads to long-term changes in global and regional climate patterns, or *climate change*.

carbon-neutral—releasing no carbon dioxide into the air

carpool—commute with others in one vehicle, reducing the number of cars on the road

car- and ride-sharing—connect people with a vehicle or a ride. Car-sharing matches people who need a car with people or companies who have one available, allowing them to rent the vehicle for shorter periods of time than traditional rental companies do. Ride-sharing connects people who want to share a ride with people who need one. Both kinds of service reduce the number of cars on the road and the need for parking, and increase use of other forms of transportation.

Ciclovía—a time when certain roads are closed off to cars so people can bike, walk or dance safely. Ciclovía in Bogotá, Colombia, is the biggest recreation event in the world, and other cities have followed its example.

congestion tax—a fee to drive into the city during busy times, charged to curb traffic and pollution and encourage people to take public transit, carpool or drive at off-peak times. Money raised from the tax supports cleaner-air initiatives and public transportation.

density—the number of people living in a particular urban area. In high-density areas, buildings are often taller or closer together to increase the number of people who can occupy a certain amount of space.

electric vehicles—cars that run on electricity, stored in a rechargeable battery. They don't burn gas or emit carbon dioxide.

Environmental Protection Agency—an organization established by the US federal government in 1970 to help protect the health of people and the environment

greenhouse gas emissions—substances released into the air when hydrocarbons such as oil and natural gas are burned. Greenhouse gases include carbon dioxide, methane and nitrous oxide, which all contribute to climate change.

gridlock—a traffic jam that prevents vehicles from moving in any direction

horsepower—a measure of the power of an engine. The higher the horsepower, the faster a car can accelerate.

Hoy No Circula (No-Driving Day)—a strategy used by some cities, such as Mexico City, to reduce traffic congestion by restricting cars from roads on certain days, based on license-plate numbers

hybrid vehicle—a vehicle that uses an electric motor and a gasoline engine to move

hyperloop—a new kind of train that will travel at super-fast speeds and take passengers from one major city to another in minutes rather than hours

idling—letting a car engine run when you're not driving

intelligent transportation systems—advanced information and communication technology systems used to minimize traffic problems, increase safety and reduce commute times

low-emission zone (LEZ)—a defined area in which polluting vehicles are restricted or deterred from entering. Many cities are creating them—or even ultra-low-emission zones—to help keep the air in those areas cleaner. Anyone who enters in a vehicle that doesn't meet emission standards is charged a fee.

nitrogen oxides—nitric oxide and nitrogen dioxide, two gases that contribute to air pollution, smog and acid rain

pollution—the presence or introduction of harmful or poisonous materials in the natural environment

reclaiming the streets—closing streets to vehicles so people can use them for recreation. It reduces traffic and pollution in certain areas or at certain times.

rush hour—a period considered the busiest time to drive, usually in the morning and evening, when most people are traveling to and from work. The roads and highways can get jammed with traffic.

smart cities—cities that use sensors, data, cameras and other technology to make traffic flow better so people can get where they need to go faster

superblocks—neighborhoods in which vehicles are banned. Traffic is routed around these areas, allowing people to use the streets.

toxic—poisonous or extremely harmful

traffic—cars and trucks, pedestrians, ships, planes and trains moving on a road, route or through an area

walking school bus—kids who walk to school together or with an adult—a great mode of active transportation

zero-emission vehicles—vehicles that don't emit carbon dioxide or other harmful gases. They can be electric or hybrid (while in battery mode).

Index

Page numbers in **bold** indicate an image caption.

Index (continued)

Acknowledgments

I consulted numerous groups and individuals for help with *Rush Hour*, from traffic experts to writing gurus. They include Professor Shoshanna Saxe and Pat Doherty from the University of Toronto; Jennifer Banks and Hong Huo from the City of Scottsdale, Arizona; Nils Hofmann and Nikki Jones, formerly of Local Motors; Professor Lina Kattan from the University of Calgary; Gideon Forman from the David Suzuki Foundation; Professor David Levinson from the University of Sydney; and Valentina Lotti and Dr. Diana Silva from King's College London.

Thank you as well to all the following people, who helped highlight the initiatives of students in their districts for chapter 4: Deborah Carlino from Martin Elementary; Theresa Vallez-Kelly from Safe Routes to School; Jeff Anderson, Charlene Lee and Nancy Pullen-Seufert from the National Center for Safe Routes to School. Thanks also to Wallace Beaton from Green Communities Canada, who helped put me in touch with Sanjana Sharma and Carolyn Williams-Noren. Josh Fullan from Maximum City spoke to me about his amazing work consulting with kids. I appreciate the Local Motors team for telling me about their work, and all the experts who chatted with me about their jobs and their research and explained all the innovations we can look forward to in the future.

Scott, thanks for reading every draft and providing such thoughtful, detailed feedback and especially for making the chapter about electric vehicles and the future of transportation more fun! Shelley and Emma, thanks for reading an early draft and providing feedback. Thanks to Gwynn Scheltema and Ruth E. Walker of Writescape for an amazing first-chapter critique. You really helped shape the tone of the book and always help me get things right! Finally, thanks also to Kirstie Hudson at Orca and everyone on the Orca team for giving me the "green light" to write this book and creating a product that will be helpful to the next generation of drivers, including my own kids.

JUSTINE APPLE

ERIN SILVER is a children's author and freelance writer with 20 years of professional industry experience. Her books include *Just Watch Me, What Kids Did: Stories of Kindness and Invention in the Time of COVID-19* and *Proud to Play: Canadian LGBTQ+ Athletes Who Made History.* Erin's work has appeared in everything from *Good Housekeeping* to the *Globe and Mail,* among others. She has a master of fine arts in creative nonfiction from the University of King's College in Halifax, Nova Scotia, a postgraduate journalism degree from Ryerson University and a bachelor of arts from the University of Toronto. Erin lives with her family in Toronto.